NITTY-GRITTY

GROSSOLOGY

OVER 101 DISGUSTING FACTS!

BY
SYLVIA BRANZEI

ILLUSTRATED BY
JACK KEELY

GROSSET & DUNLAP

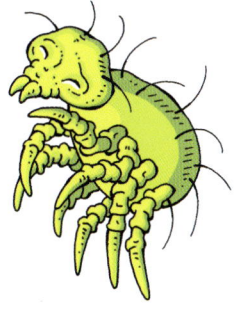

GROSSET & DUNLAP
An imprint of Penguin Random House LLC
1745 Broadway, New York, New York 10019

First published in the United States of America by Grosset & Dunlap,
an imprint of Penguin Random House LLC, 2025

GROSSET & DUNLAP and GROSSOLOGY
are registered trademarks of Penguin Random House LLC.

Visit us online at penguinrandomhouse.com.

Library of Congress Cataloging-in-Publication Data is available.

Manufactured in China

ISBN 9780593752432   10 9 8 7 6 5 4 3 2 1 TOPL

Design by Kimberley Sampson

A GROSS INTRODUCTION

Grossology is the study of really gross things. Factoids are interesting little bits of information. This is a little book of interesting and icky information.

After reading this book, you will not be the same. You will begin to appreciate the disgusting stuff that surrounds you. And you will be excited to share what you find out with everyone you know! You will be a step closer to becoming a grossologist, or a person who studies putrid things.

What are you waiting for?
Turn the page and start getting gross!

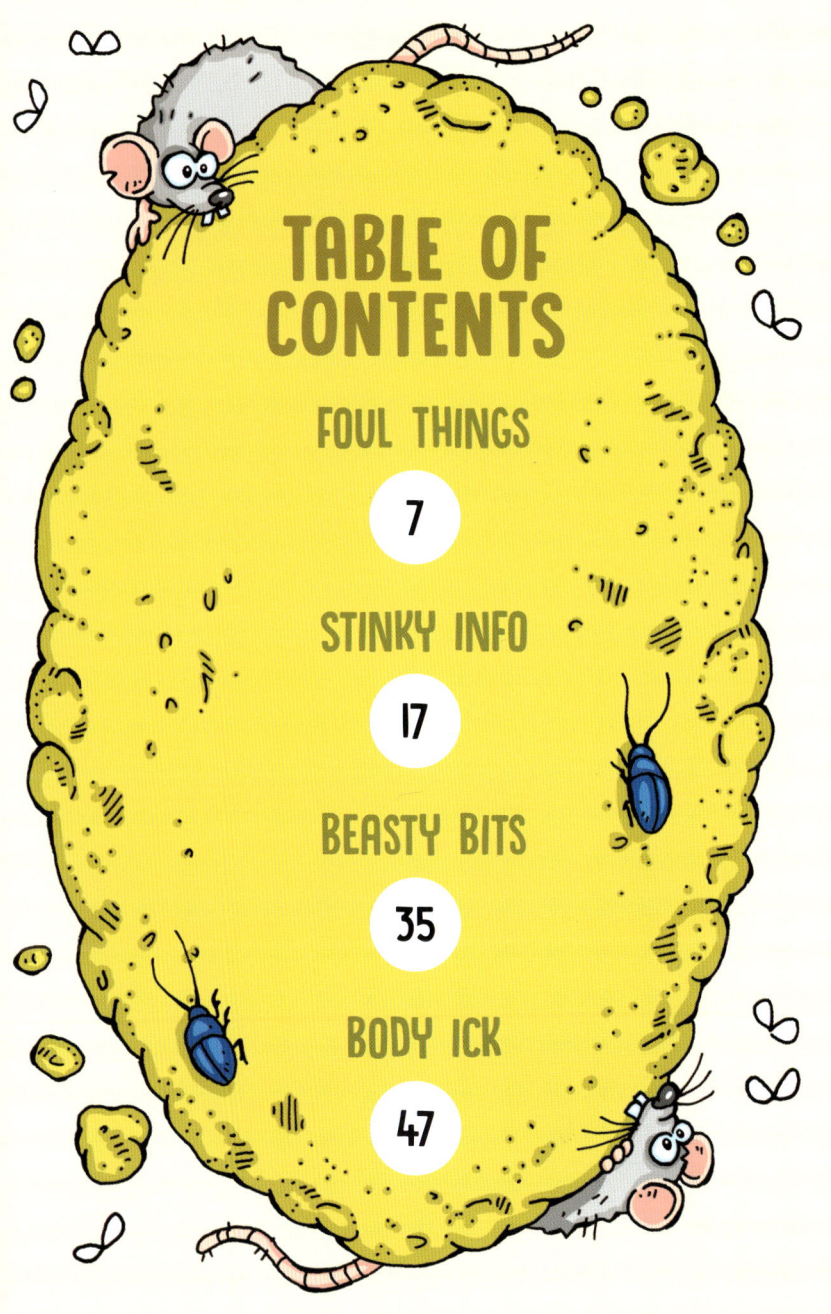

TABLE OF CONTENTS

FOUL THINGS
DOOKIE

SEVENTY-FIVE-MILLION-YEAR-OLD TURDS LEFT BY A TWENTY-FOUR-FOOT-LONG HADROSAUR MEASURED MORE THAN A FOOT WIDE AND ALMOST TEN INCHES TALL.

- Middens are generations of pack rat poo, urine, and den garbage. A midden looks like a chunky chocolate bar. They look so yummy, a group of miners traveling to California during the 1849 Gold Rush tried eating them.

- Processed bird poop and urine can be used to make explosives. *Coo-BOOM!*

- A man named Frank Hill once made and sold jewelry out of quail droppings encased in plastic.

- Diapers for birds were invented in 1959. You can still buy them today!

DIGEST THIS!

DINNER CAN HANG OUT IN YOUR STOMACH FOR FIVE HOURS!

- It takes your body a day and a half for a tuna fish sandwich to go from your mouth to the toilet bowl.

- The path food travels from your mouth to your butthole is about twenty-five feet!

- If you tell someone to touch their stomach, they will often put their hand on their intestines. Your stomach is actually above your belly button and your intestines are below it.

10

FARTS

SCIENTISTS IN ANTARCTICA DISCOVERED THAT WHALES FART. THEY DON'T KNOW HOW OFTEN, BUT THEY DO KNOW THAT THE FARTS ARE REALLY BIG!

- Little critters called yeast are put into bread dough. When the yeast eat the dough, they fart. The yeast's fart gas makes bread dough rise.

- Korean for fart is *bang gwi.*

- *Pukat'.* That's what you do if you are in Russia and you fart.

- In Yiddish, farts are called *fartsn.*

PEE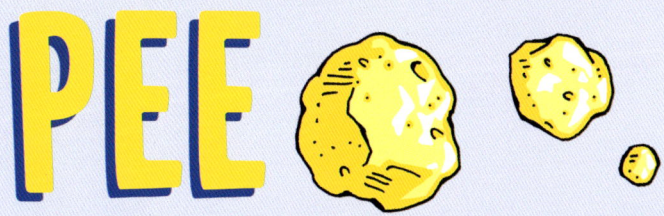

THE NEXT TIME YOU PEE, TRY TO HOLD YOUR BREATH. THAT MAKES IT ALMOST IMPOSSIBLE TO PEE BECAUSE THE SHEET OF MUSCLE UNDER THE LUNGS CAN'T PRESS DOWN. THAT MUSCLE HELPS YOU EMPTY YOUR BLADDER.

- People who drink a lot of coffee, cola, or tea often feel like they have to pee, although there is only a little bit of urine in their bladder. This is because caffeine contracts the bladder muscles, so you feel the need to pee.

- During the 1600s in England, several quacks told people that they knew the secret of turning pee into gold.

- A female's urethra, or pee pee delivery tube, is about one and a half inches long. A male's urethra is about eight inches long.

CRAPPERS

THE PERSON CREDITED WITH INVENTING THE FLUSHING TOILET WAS NAMED SIR JOHN HARINGTON. HE CALLED HIS TOILET AJAX BUT THAT NAME DIDN'T CATCH ON.

- Before the 1850s, there were very few indoor toilets. Chamber pots filled with pee and poo were dumped from the window onto the street. "Look out below!" *Splat!*

- The modern flushing toilet has a stink trap that stops sewer smells from seeping up into the toilet.

- In England during the Tudor period, the Groom of the Stool had the very important job of tending to the king's needs as he relieved himself on the royal stool.

15

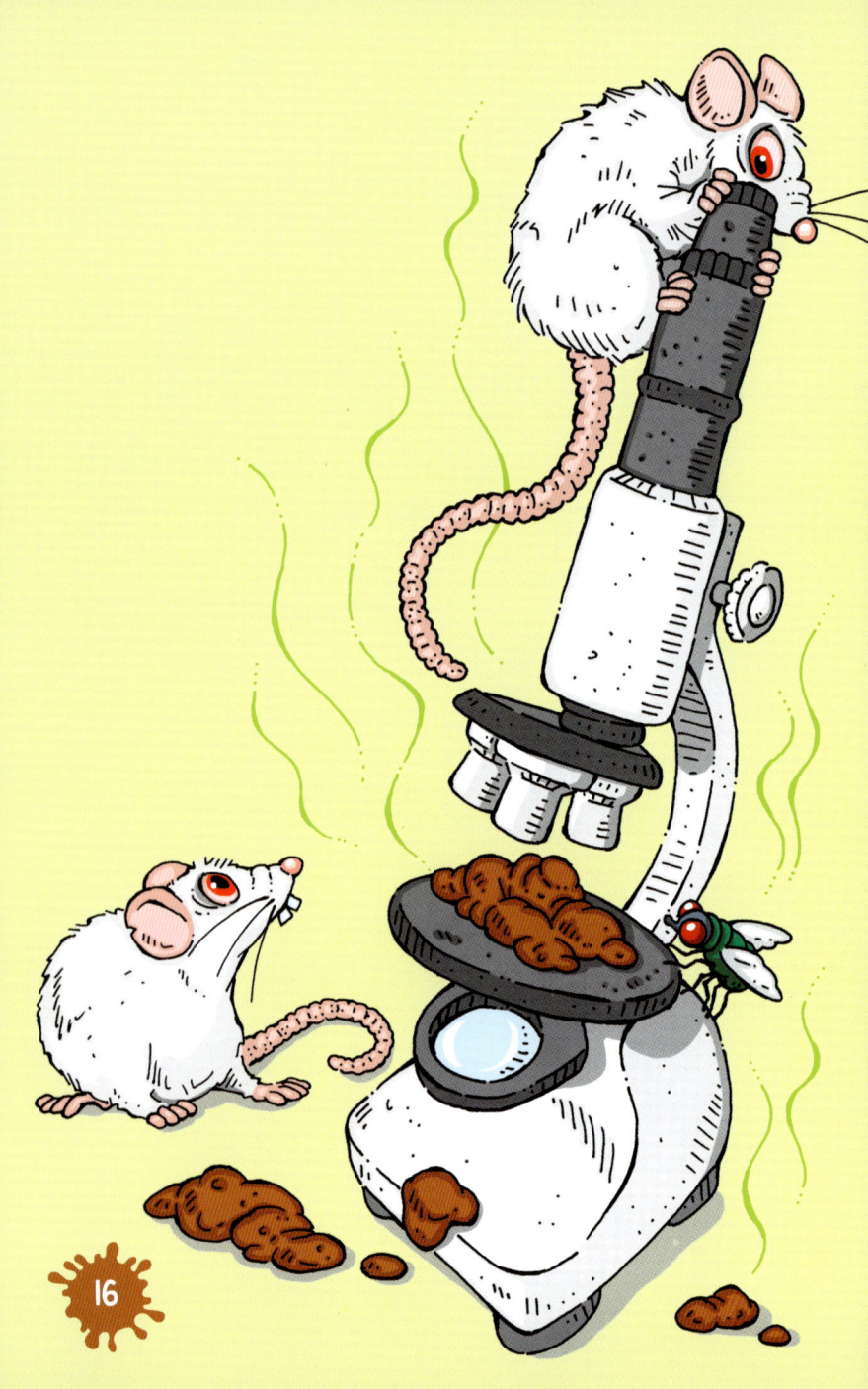

STINKY INFO

SCAT

SCATOLOGY IS THE STUDY OF POOP. IT IS ALSO CALLED COPROLOGY.

- A coprolite is fossilized dookie.

- Scatomancy is the art of fortune-telling by studying poop.

- Scatologists are experts who study animal feces, or scat. *Feces* is the scientific word for poop.

- Scat field guides are handy books that help budding scatologists identify wild animal dookie.

GIRAFFES

ALTHOUGH GIRAFFES ARE VERY TALL, THEIR POOPS ARE VERY SMALL. THEY ARE ABOUT THE SIZE OF LARGE MARBLES.

- Giraffes only eat plants; their poops don't stink too much.

- A giraffe drops about thirty-three pounds of pellets a day. Now that is a big pile of marble-size poops.

- An American returning from Kenya brought home giraffe droppings that she planned to make into a necklace. Customs officials took away her poopy souvenir.

- The daily output of giraffe pee is about five gallons.

19

LIONS

AFRICAN LIONS MARK THEIR TERRITORY BY LEAVING THEIR DOOKIE OUT FOR OTHER ANIMALS TO SMELL AND SEE.

- Since scat can tell a lot about the health of a lion, zookeepers will sometimes mix specific colored glitter into the food of each lion. That way they can match the sparkly poo to each individual pooper.

- Since lions are meat eaters, their large poops contain fur, bones, and sometimes feathers.

HIPPOS

MALE HIPPOS DEFEND THEIR TERRITORY WITH POO. THEY SWING THEIR TAILS IN THE WATER WHILE POOPING AND PEEING TO SPRAY THEIR SCENT (AND EVERYTHING ELSE) AROUND.

- Hippos usually go number two in the water.

- Hippo poop is about the size of a small bowling ball.

- One type of leech specializes in hippo blood. Since hippos have thick skin, the leech lives and feeds in the hippo's rectum, or poo poo hole.

OSTRICHES

OSTRICHES ARE THE ONLY LIVING BIRDS WHOSE POOP IS SEPARATE FROM THEIR PEE.

- Ostrich poo comes in various shapes and sometimes it looks like a large chocolate Kiss.

- Ostriches have a very long intestine. It takes about thirty-six hours for their food to take the trip through.

- Ostriches urinate then defecate, which is a fancy way of saying that they pee before they poo.

25

GORILLAS

GORILLAS EAT DOOKIE. THIS IS CALLED COPROPHAGY.

- Munching poo snacks helps gorillas take in important nutrients and bacteria.

- Gorilla poo is sausage-shaped, kind of like a large Tootsie Roll.

- Sometimes gorillas and chimps in zoos will throw turds at visitors. Some researchers studied dookie-tossing chimps and concluded that those who threw more stools had better-developed brains in the areas of motor skills and communication.

RABBITS

RABBITS MAKE TWO KINDS OF DOOKIE: A DRY ROUND PELLET AND A SQUISHY GLOSSY POOP CALLED CECOTROPES.

- Rabbits eat their cecotropes. They do this in order to get all the nutrients they need. A healthy bunny is a poo-eating bunny.

- An average-size bunny will release 200 to 300 poops every day.

- A rabbit with a poopy bottom could get fly strike. Fly strike is when a fly lays eggs in the butt mess. The eggs hatch and the rabbit becomes overrun with maggots.

COWS

A SINGLE DAIRY COW CAN RELEASE A HUNDRED OR MORE POUNDS OF MANURE EVERY DAY.

- A single cow delivers almost twenty tons of cow pies every year. *Plop, plop, plop.*

- In some parts of the world, people use dried cow dung for cooking fires.

- A cow poos every ninety to one hundred twenty minutes.

ELEPHANTS

AN ELEPHANT CAN DEPOSIT MORE THAN
FIVE GALLONS OF DOOKIE IN A SINGLE DUMP.
THAT'S A BIG PIE!

- One elephant poops eight to ten times a day. Over a year that's about forty tons of dookie!

- The most expensive coffee in the world is elephant dung coffee. Coffee beans are fed to an elephant, who plops out the digested beans along with the doo-doo. The beans are collected and made into a smooth brew.

TAPEWORMS

TAPEWORMS USUALLY TAKE UP RESIDENCE IN THE INTESTINES. THEY ENTER A BODY IN EGG FORM WHEN SOMEONE EATS UNDERCOOKED MEAT, GETS EXPOSED TO ANIMAL DOOKIE, OR DRINKS UNSAFE WATER. THEY GROW IN THE INTESTINE INTO A LONG RIBBONLIKE WORM.

- A Japanese scientist who studied parasites once swallowed tapeworm eggs on purpose. He even named the tapeworm living in his intestines.

- In parts of Africa, tapeworms are so common that more than half of the people in some villages have one living in their gut.

- A tapeworm can grow as long as a medium-size school bus—thirty feet long!

LEECHES

A LEECH IS A BLOODSUCKING WORM. SOME PEOPLE JUST CALL THEM BLOODSUCKERS.

- Imagine this: Leeches on your temples to cure a headache! This was a cure hundreds of years ago. And it is being used again today for some migraine headache sufferers.

- *Leech* is actually a very old English word for *physician*. For centuries, people thought leeches cured a person from most any ailment by sucking out the bad blood.

- Giant leeches can reach the length of your arm!

TURKEY VULTURES

TURKEY VULTURES DINE ON ROTTEN MEAT
BECAUSE THEY CAN'T TEAR FRESH MEAT
WITH THEIR WEAK BEAKS.

- They have bald heads, so the rotten meat doesn't get stuck to the head when plunged into a carcass.

- When turkey vultures are startled, they spew all over the intruder. The rotten meat vomit smells terrible.

- Turkey vultures poop on their own legs to keep themselves cool—and stop attacks from parasites and bacteria.

- A turkey vulture can smell rotting flesh from over a mile away.

HAGFISH

HAGFISH OOZE A SUBSTANCE CALLED MUCIN THAT GETS THICKER IN WATER. IF DISTURBED, A HAGFISH CAN TURN A FIVE-GALLON BUCKET OF SEAWATER INTO A BUCKET FULL OF SLIME.

- Hagfish are also called slime eels, snot snakes, and slime hags.

- Slime eels eat by going up the butthole, gills, eye, or mouth of sickly or dead fish. Then they eat them from the inside out.

- Hagfish are the only fish that sneeze! They do this to prevent choking on their own slime.

NAKED MOLE RATS

NAKED MOLE RATS ARE ALMOST COMPLETELY HAIRLESS EXCEPT FOR TINY WHISKERS IN AND OUTSIDE THEIR MOUTHS AND BETWEEN THEIR TOES.

- Naked mole rats are almost blind.

- You can see the organs inside a newborn naked mole rat.

- Naked mole rats are also called sand puppies.

- Naked mole rat babies, or pups, eat poop from the adults. The feces are rich in nutrients and gut microbes.

VAMPIRE BATS

A VAMPIRE BAT DRINKS A COUPLE OF SPOONFULS OF BLOOD EVERY NIGHT. OVER A YEAR THAT IS ALMOST THREE GALLONS OF YUMMY BLOOD.

- A well-fed vampire bat will share a meal by vomiting bloody barf into the mouth of a hungry cave mate.

- In one year, a colony of one hundred vampire bats could completely drain the blood from more than twenty-five cows.

- Vampire bat spit contains a chemical that stops blood from clotting. The chemical is called Draculin. Yes, it was named after Count Dracula.

BODY ICK
TEETH

AFTER THE LOSS OF HER FRONT TEETH, QUEEN ELIZABETH I APPEARED IN PUBLIC WITH A CLOTH STUFFED INTO HER MOUTH.

- The ancient Egyptians invented toothpaste more than 4,000 years ago. It was made with vinegar and ground rock.

- In the 1800s, people used tooth powder made of ground-up burned eggshells and fish scales.

- Your teeth started growing more than three months before you were even born.

BARF

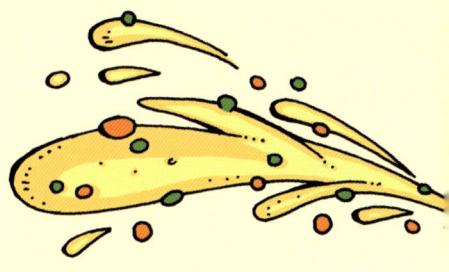

A MOTHER WOLF GORGES ON THE MEAT OF A FRESH KILL. SHE RETURNS TO HER PUPS AND BARFS IT OUT FOR THE HUNGRY LITTLE ONES TO LAP UP.

- The invention of barf was an accident. Some guy was working on a new type of plastic toy. When cleaning up spilled plastic, he noticed the junk made it look like barf. His mistake became the ever-popular fake barf.

- Here are some phrases for throwing up: toss your cookies, spill your guts, lose your lunch, and feed the fish.

SPIT

CHEWING TOBACCO WAS COMMON IN EARLY AMERICA. SINCE CHEWERS SPIT A LOT, POTS WERE PLACED INDOORS FOR THEM TO SPIT INTO. THE SPIT POTS WERE CALLED SPITTOONS.

- Fish don't make saliva because they only eat moist food.

- Without saliva, food would have no taste. You can't taste anything unless it can be dissolved in the saliva on your tongue.

- In some states and cities in the United States, it is illegal to spit on the sidewalk.

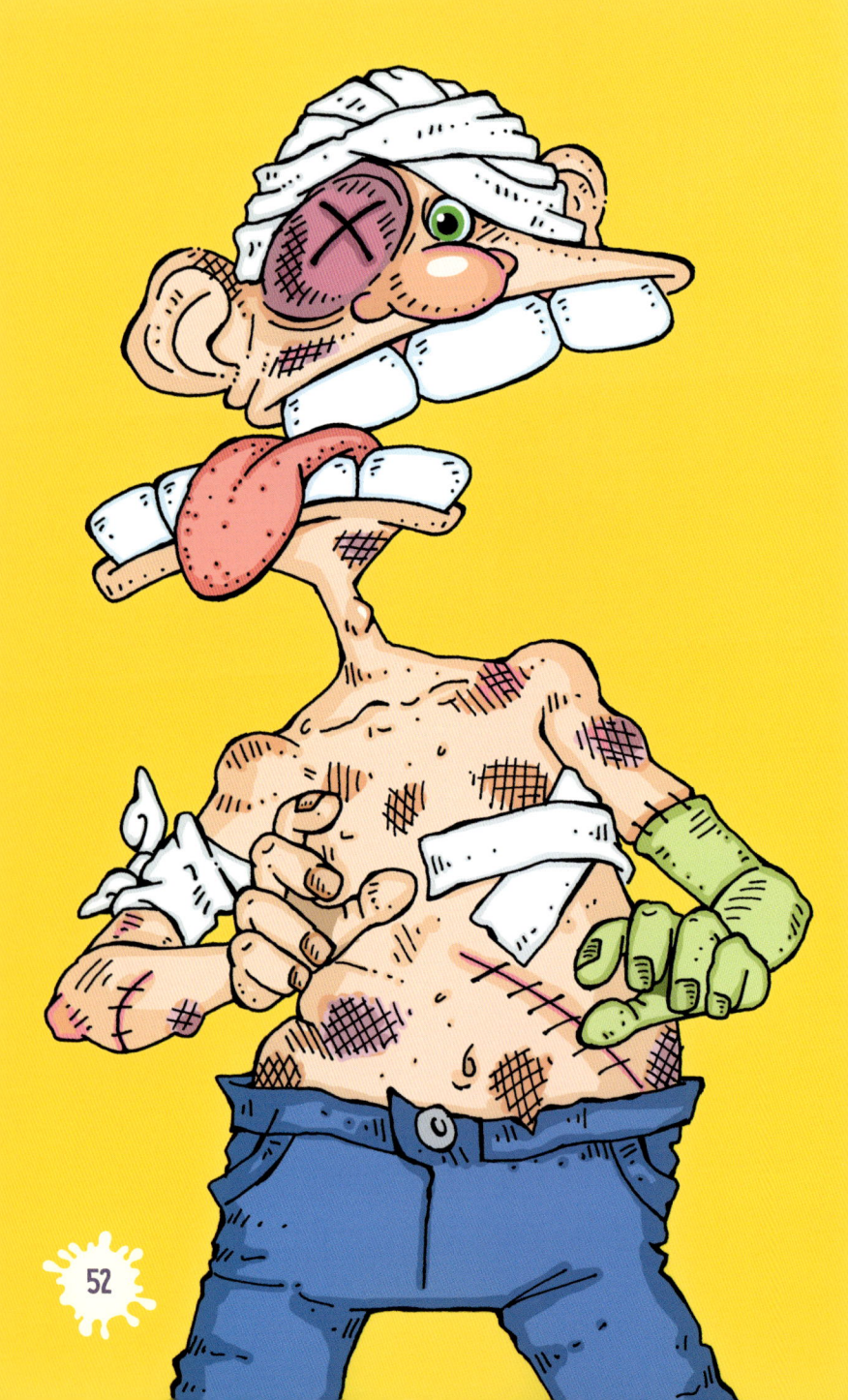

SCAB

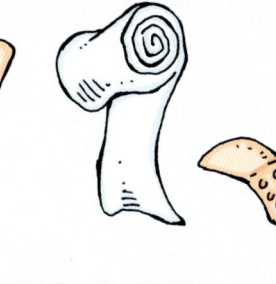

A SCAR SOMETIMES FORMS AFTER A CUT HEALS. THAT'S BECAUSE THE NEW SKIN THAT YOUR BODY MAKES IS LESS FLEXIBLE.

- You should change a bandage daily to keep a cut clean.

- If you get a small cut, it will take four to eight minutes for your body to halt the bleeding.

- The word *scab* comes from the Latin word *scabere*, which means "to scratch."

- Although tempting, you should never ever pick at a scab. Scab picking slows healing and may cause infection.

SWEAT

TO SAY THAT SOMEONE "SWEATS LIKE A HOG" IS VERY UNFAIR TO PIGS. PIGS DON'T EVEN SWEAT. HUMANS HAVE MORE SWEAT GLANDS THAN ANY OTHER MAMMAL.

- Some people are born not being able to sweat. This condition, called anhidrosis, is very rare.

- The little bit of sweat on your palms and fingers helps you to grip objects.

- Hockey players lose five to eight pounds of water weight in one game.

- You are born with a set number of sweat glands. As you grow, your sweat glands get farther and farther apart.

SKIN

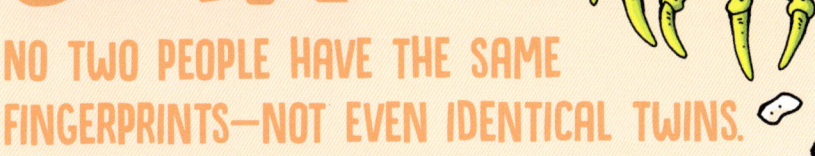

- The waxes and oils in your skin contain chemicals that can kill some germs.

- Right now, over two million bacteria are living on your chin, cheeks, and nose. That is more bacteria than there are people living in Nebraska.

- You shed about seventy-seven pounds of skin cells in your lifetime. Millions of dust mites in your bed, rug, and sofa are chowing down right now on skin cells that you sloughed off last night.

SNOT

A LONG TIME AGO, PEOPLE THOUGHT THAT SNOT RUNNING FROM YOUR NOSE BECAUSE OF A COLD VIRUS WAS ACTUALLY YOUR BRAIN LEAKING.

- Your snot has chemicals in it that kill some germs.

- You make about a liter of snot every day. And you swallow most of it. Tiny hairs move dirty mucus to the back of your throat. *Gulp!* The icky mucus then goes into your stomach, where the acids destroy the germs in the snot.

BRAIN

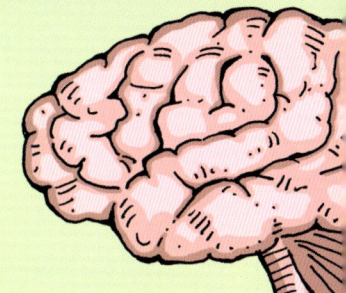

- Brains are actually soft and squishy, kind of like Jell-O.

- In 2023, an Australian woman underwent brain surgery. The surgeons found a live roundworm wriggling around in her brain! The type of roundworm living in her brain is usually only found in pythons. Doctors think she may have swallowed the worm eggs from eating grasses infected with python poop.

- Your brain is nearly 60 percent fat!

MUMMIES

IN ANCIENT EGYPT, EMBALMERS REMOVED THE BRAIN FROM A BODY BY SHOVING A HOOK UP THE NOSE, TWIRLING IT AROUND, THEN LETTING THE BRAIN MUSH LEAK OUT OF THE NOSE.

- In Europe during the 1500s, people carried around little pouches of ground-up mummy as a cure for bruises, bloody noses, and pretty much anything that ailed them.

- From the 1600s until the 1920s, artists used a pigment called mummy brown in their painting. Yep, it was made from ground-up mummies.

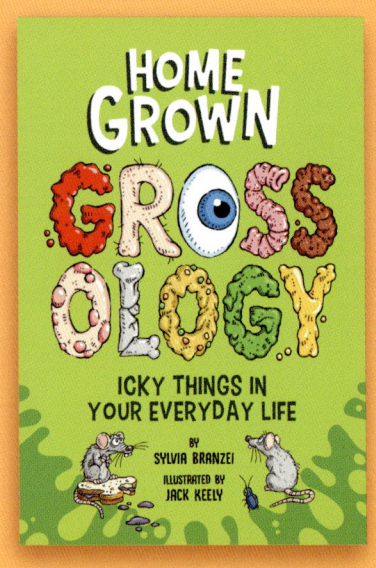
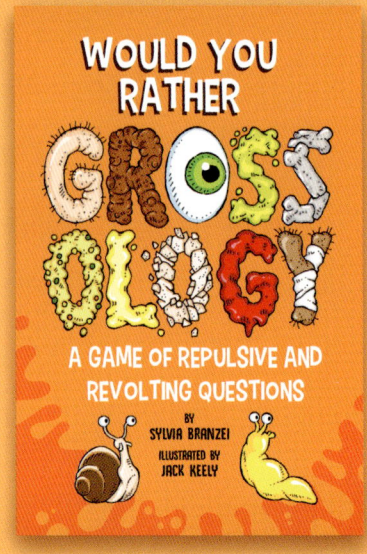